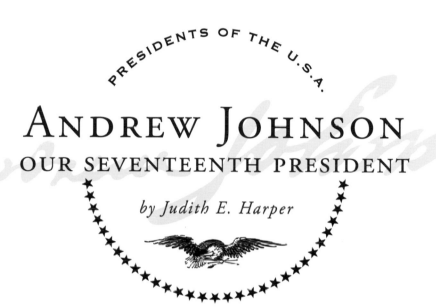

ANDREW JOHNSON
OUR SEVENTEENTH PRESIDENT

by Judith E. Harper

THE CHILD'S WORLD®

THE CHILD'S WORLD®
1980 Lookout Drive • Mankato, MN 56003-1705
800-599-READ • www.childsworld.com

ACKNOWLEDGMENTS
The Child's World®: Mary Berendes, Publishing Director

The Creative Spark: Mary McGavic, Project Director and Page Production;
Shari Joffe, Editorial Director; Deborah Goodsite, Photo Research

The Design Lab: Kathleen Petelinsek, Design

Content Adviser: Andrew Johnson National Historic Site, Greeneville, Tennessee

PHOTOS
Cover and page 3: National Portrait Gallery, Smithsonian Institution/Art Resource

Interior: Alamy: 18 and 38 (Visual Arts Library (London)); Courtesy of the
American Antiquarian Society: 23; Courtesy of the Andrew Johnson National
Historic Site, Greeneville, Tennessee: 4, 9 top, 9 bottom, 19 and 39, 25; The Art
Archive/National Archives Washington DC: 22; The Bridgeman Art Library: 14
(Private Collection/Peter Newark American Pictures), 17, 21 (Chicago Historical
Museum), 34 (Private Collection/Peter Newark American Pictures); Corbis: 29,
36 (Bettmann); Kevin Davidson Illustration: 7, 15; Getty Images: 26 (Getty
Images), 37 bottom (Hulton Archive); The Granger Collection, New York: 8, 12,
24 and 38, 31, 33, 35; The Image Works: 10 (Jeff Greenberg); iStockphoto: 44
(Tim Fan); Library of Congress, Prints and Photographs Division: 32, 37 top;
SuperStock, Inc.: 5 (SuperStock), 30 (Culver Pictures, Inc.); U.S. Air Force photo: 45.

LIBRARY OF CONGRESS CATALOGING-IN-PUBLICATION DATA
Harper, Judith E., 1953–
  Andrew Johnson / by Judith E. Harper.
    p. cm. — (Presidents of the U.S.A.)
  Includes bibliographical references and index.
  ISBN 978-1-60253-046-1 (library bound : alk. paper)
  1. Johnson, Andrew, 1808-1875—Juvenile literature. 2. Presidents—United
States—Biography—Juvenile literature. I. Title.
  E667.H369 2008
  973.8'1092 dc22
  [B]
                                    2007042609

Printed in the United States of America
Mankato, Minnesota
November, 2012
PA02153

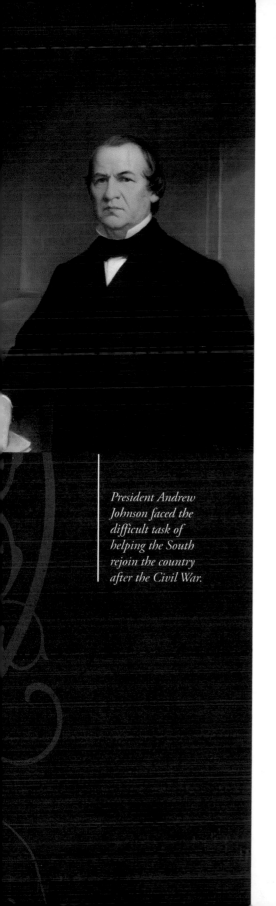

President Andrew
Johnson faced the
difficult task of
helping the South
rejoin the country
after the Civil War.

TABLE OF CONTENTS

POVERTY AND AMBITION

The United States faced a huge crisis in 1860. The country was drawing closer to a civil war between the Northern and Southern states. A civil war occurs when citizens of the same country battle one another. On December 20, South Carolina became the first state to **secede** from the United States. Tennessee Senator Andrew Johnson bravely stood up to speak to his fellow Southern senators. He pleaded with them to persuade their states to remain in the Union, another name for the United States. Johnson was the only Southern senator to urge the Southern states not to secede. He said, "I [beg] every man throughout the nation who is a patriot … to come forward … and swear by our God … that the **Constitution** shall be saved, and the Union preserved."

Andrew Johnson became the U.S. president after President Lincoln died.

In 1865, after the Civil War was over, Andrew Johnson became president. He vowed to reunite the country and to protect the Constitution. This was a difficult job in a nation that had been ripped apart by war. He tried to achieve this goal in his own way. He was convinced that his way was right, even when Congress and his advisors told him he was wrong. When Congress tried to force Johnson to leave the presidency, he fought back. He remained president until the end of his term. This is the story of the first American president to be **impeached** by Congress.

On December 29, 1808, Andrew Johnson was born in a two-room cabin in Raleigh, North Carolina.

Johnson was born in this simple cabin in Raleigh, North Carolina, in 1808.

5

Jacob Johnson died a hero. He collapsed shortly after saving three men from drowning.

An educated man often read aloud to the apprentices and workers in James Selby's tailor shop. Andrew Johnson's favorite book was filled with the speeches of famous American and English leaders. He treasured these speeches so much that the man gave the book to him.

His parents were poor, hardworking people. His father, Jacob Johnson, worked at a bank, keeping the rooms clean. He also served as a city **constable.** Andrew's mother, Mary Johnson, worked as a seamstress and laundress.

Andrew was just three years old when his father died. The Johnsons faced hard times after that. Mary's earnings were not enough to keep them from hunger. She remarried in 1814, but her new husband was not a good provider. The family slipped deeper into poverty.

Andrew had a deep longing for learning but never attended school. There were no public schools available, and his family could not afford to pay for a private school. This did not stop Andrew. He learned to read while he and his older brother William were **apprentices** to a tailor named James Selby. Of course, Andrew also learned the sewing skills that a tailor needed to know.

When Andrew was 15 years old, he and William ran away. They did this even though they had promised to stay with Selby until they completed their apprenticeships. But the boys were in trouble for throwing rocks at a neighbor's house, and they didn't want to be punished. So Andrew and William walked to South Carolina, where they found work as tailors. Andrew then spent several years moving from one village to the next. He was always sure to find a job because he was such a fine tailor.

In 1826, Andrew settled in the mountains of East Tennessee. He later went to live in the village of

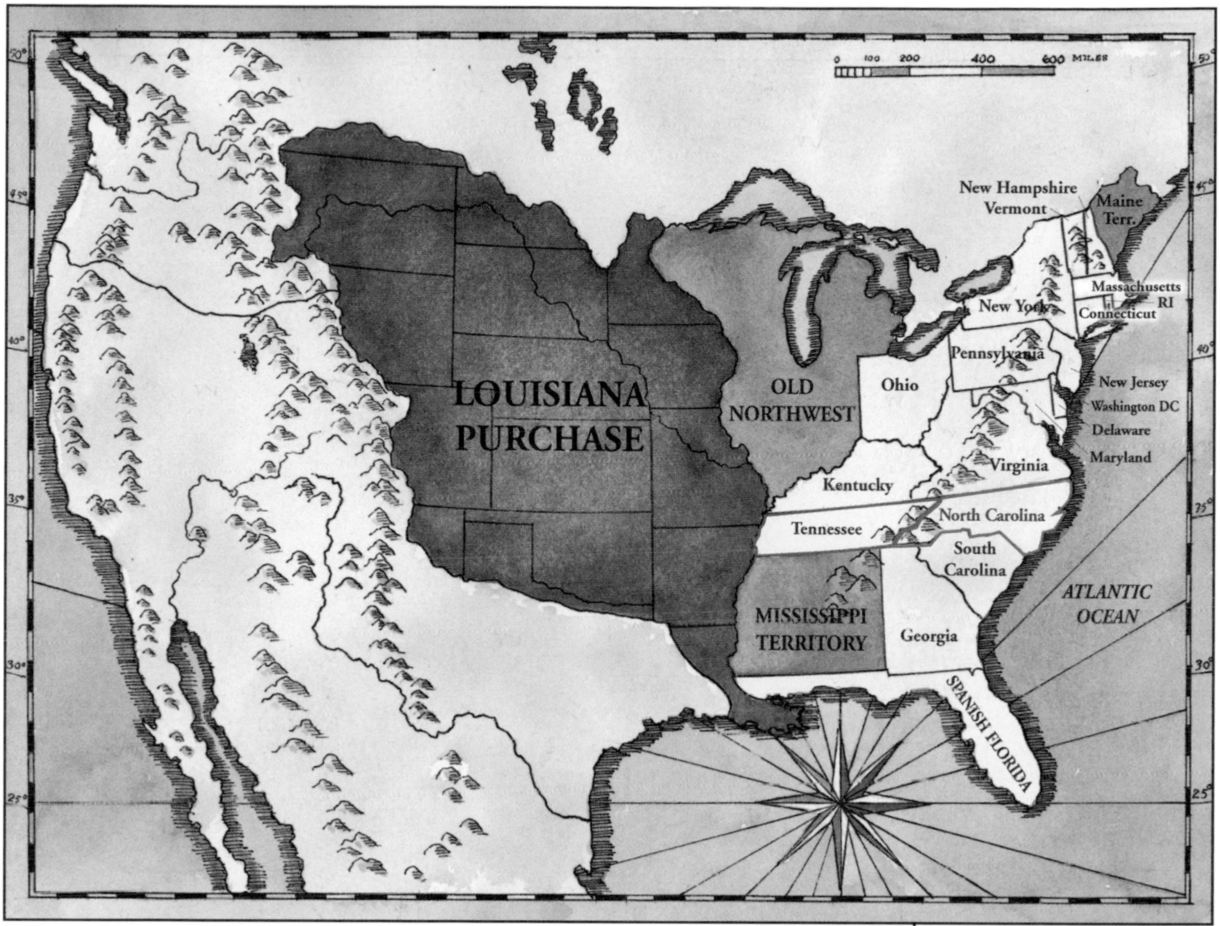
0 100 200 400 600 MILES
LOUISIANA PURCHASE
OLD NORTHWEST
Ohio
New Hampshire
Vermont
Maine Terr.
Massachusetts
RI
Connecticut
New York
Pennsylvania
New Jersey
Washington DC
Delaware
Maryland
Virginia
Kentucky
Tennessee
North Carolina
South Carolina
Georgia
MISSISSIPPI TERRITORY
SPANISH FLORIDA
ATLANTIC OCEAN

Greeneville. There he met Eliza McCardle. Eliza was fatherless, too.

She and her mother were quilt and sandal makers. Andrew and Eliza were attracted to each other immediately. Within a year, they were married. She was 16 years old, and he was 18.

Andrew Johnson soon opened his own successful tailor shop. He employed a number of tailors, and his business grew. As he earned money, he bought property, which increased his wealth. He owned a large home across the street from his tailoring business. He also was able to afford a farm for his

This map shows the United States around the time that Andrew Johnson was born. Johnson was a Southerner. He was originally from North Carolina but moved to Tennessee in 1826. Although he worked in the nation's capital for many years, he always considered Tennessee his home.

Before he became a politician, Johnson was a successful tailor. This engraving shows the tailor shop in Greeneville, Tennessee, that he owned.

mother and stepfather to live on. Eventually, he sold his business and invested the money he gained by buying more land and buildings. By this time, he was considered wealthy.

Andrew and Eliza had a happy marriage. Between 1828 and 1852, Eliza gave birth to three sons and two daughters. In their early years, Eliza helped Andrew improve his writing and arithmetic. She had been lucky enough to go to school. Andrew loved books and read whenever he had the time.

In 1829, Andrew Johnson was elected alderman in Greeneville. An alderman is a person who helps to make the laws of a city. He and the rest of the aldermen made the laws for the community. Johnson was reelected to serve in this position several times. Each victory inspired him to go further in **politics.** He wanted to hold other, more important positions. Between 1834 and 1843, he served two terms as mayor of Greeneville and was elected three times to the Tennessee **state legislature,** which met in Nashville, the state capital. He served in both parts of the state legislature, the assembly and the senate.

As a state lawmaker, Andrew Johnson supported laws dealing with education. He also worked to make sure that the state government did not interfere with people's businesses. Other lawmakers listened whenever Johnson spoke his mind. He was known as an important leader in state government. A Nashville newspaper said, "We consider [Johnson] … among the first men of the

Andrew Johnson never attended school. His wife, Eliza, taught him to write and do arithmetic and helped him with his reading skills.

Johnson bought property with the money he earned in his tailor shop. This house in Greeneville was his home for 24 years.

state. He is just the man for a crisis. Bold, prompt, and energetic, … no obstacles discourage him."

As a politician, Andrew Johnson's greatest cause was to help ordinary working people—farmers, craftspeople, and laborers. The state legislature was full of rich and well-educated men. Johnson believed it was his duty to make laws that would help people who were not wealthy. When he spoke to crowds of working people in East Tennessee, he told them that they, not the rich, were the most important citizens in the United States. He said that the labor of working people made the United States a powerful nation.

ANDREW JOHNSON'S ELECTED OFFICES

Andrew Johnson won his first election in 1829 and then held many different elected positions.

1829–1834	Alderman in Greeneville
1834	Mayor of Greeneville
1835–1837	Representative to the Tennessee state legislature
1837	Mayor of Greeneville
1839–1841	Representative to the Tennessee state legislature
1841–1843	State senator
1843–1852	Member of the U.S. House of Representatives
1853–1857	Governor of Tennessee
1857–1862	U.S. senator
1862–1865	Military governor of Tennessee
1865	Vice president (for six weeks)
1865–1869	President of the United States
1875	U.S. senator (for less than six months)

When Andrew Johnson had his own tailor shop in Greeneville, he not only hired tailors to work for him, he also employed men to read to his workers. He paid the readers fifty cents an hour.

Mordecai Lincoln, a cousin of Abraham Lincoln, lived in Greeneville. He conducted the marriage ceremony of Andrew and Eliza Johnson. Johnson and Mordecai Lincoln enjoyed **debating** each other. They also served as aldermen together.

A LOVE FOR THE SPOKEN WORD

From the time he was a tailor's apprentice, Andrew Johnson was fascinated by politics. He loved to hear the speeches of famous leaders read aloud. He wanted to become a great public speaker himself someday.

He was not alone in his passion for speechmaking. Public speaking fascinated millions of Americans in the 1800s. Listening to speeches, lectures, and sermons was as popular then as going to movies or sporting events is today.

When he was a tailor in Greeneville, Johnson had a friend with whom he often disagreed. They enjoyed debating with each other. Johnson studied and practiced his public speaking whenever he could. Soon he was spending his evenings walking four miles to and from Tusculum College so that he could participate in debates that were held there.

As a young politician in Tennessee, Johnson became known as a great speaker. He had a powerful, clear voice. He was a fighter, and his opponents knew it. With his words, he "cut and slashed right and left ... running his opponents through and through with a rusty jagged weapon." The crowds loved his toughness. His public speaking proved that Johnson was strong, intelligent, knowledgeable, and quick-thinking—exactly the qualities people wanted in a leader.

CHAPTER TWO

ON TO WASHINGTON!

For years, Andrew Johnson was an important political leader in East Tennessee. His success in politics inspired him to reach for a higher office. He decided to run for a seat in the U.S. House of Representatives in Washington, D.C. After a hard-fought campaign, he was elected in 1843.

In the House, Johnson began a long battle to help working people buy land. His own experience taught him how difficult it was for poor people to lift themselves out of poverty. He knew that land ownership helped him become successful. He believed that the government should make laws to help working people improve their lives.

Johnson worked hard to write and pass a law that would allow the head of every family to own 160 acres of government land. This **bill** was called the **Homestead** Act. Johnson struggled to make it a law while he served in the House of Representatives and later when he was in the U.S. Senate.

In 1853, after 10 years in the House, Johnson lost his reelection campaign. He returned to Tennessee. There his defeat was soon followed by another victory.

He was elected governor of Tennessee that same year. As governor, Johnson made changes that helped poor people get an education. He convinced state lawmakers to increase taxes to pay for public schools and libraries.

In 1857, the Tennessee legislature chose Johnson to be a U.S. senator. Back in Washington, he continued working on his homestead bill. In July of 1860, Congress finally approved it. To Johnson's deep disappointment, it did not become a law because President James Buchanan decided to **veto** it. The Senate then voted on the bill again. It could still become a law if two-thirds or more of the senators voted for it, but they did not. Johnson's years of effort were not wasted, however. In 1862, when he was no longer at work on the bill, a new version of the homestead act became law.

Like his fellow Southerners, Senator Johnson supported slavery. He also believed that the Constitution gave the state governments the right to govern themselves. This included the right to decide whether an individual state would allow slavery. But, as he said many times, he did not believe that states had the right to secede from the Union. This was **treason,** he declared.

In 1861, one Southern state after another seceded from the Union. Johnson rushed home to Tennessee.

In 1861, most slave states seceded from the Union to form the Confederate States of America. But four slave states decided to fight with the Union. These were called the border states because they sat on the border between the North and the South. President Lincoln and other leaders did not outlaw slavery in these states because the Union needed their support.

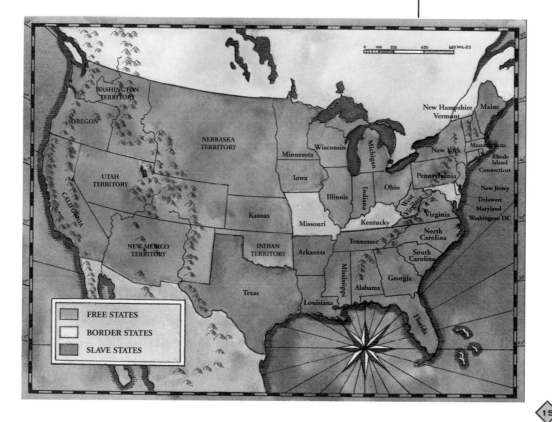

When the Confederate army invaded Unionist Greeneville, the soldiers seized Johnson's home and property. They forced his family to leave and turned his home into army housing.

Andrew Johnson tried to run for president in 1860. He hoped that he might be the Democratic Party's candidate. A bitter battle among Democrats made him decide to withdraw from the race.

He was determined to keep his home state in the Union. He gave speeches all over the state. Tempers were running high. People in support of the **Confederacy** were angry with **Unionists** like Johnson. A few threatened to **assassinate** him. The threats did not stop him. When Johnson spoke to crowds, he kept a gun with him so that he could defend himself if his life were in danger.

Many people from East Tennessee wanted to stay in the Union. Unfortunately, the rest of the state did not. Tennessee, the last Southern state to break away from the Union, seceded on June 8, 1861. With his battle for Tennessee lost, Johnson headed for safety in Kentucky, a slave state that had sided with the Union. He then traveled to Washington, D.C., where he was given a hero's welcome. He was the only Southern senator who served in the Senate after his state had seceded.

President Abraham Lincoln liked Johnson's courage, his toughness, and his devotion to the Union. He also admired Johnson's ability to stand up for what he believed. For all of these reasons, Lincoln appointed Johnson the military governor of Tennessee in 1862. Then Lincoln selected Johnson as the **candidate** for vice president in the 1864 presidential election. The two men belonged to different **political parties.** Lincoln was a **Republican,** and Johnson was a **Democrat.** But they joined forces to run in the 1864 presidential election. Their new political party was called the National Union Party. It united all Republicans and

Democrats who were Unionists. Lincoln and Johnson won the election.

All through the election season, Andrew Johnson had Tennessee's problems on his mind. Before the election, Tennessee leaders were unable to agree on and make decisions about Tennessee's future. In spite of Johnson's hard work, they were reluctant to rejoin the Union. The election victory of President Lincoln and Andrew Johnson in November 1864 helped to change their minds. Equally important, however, were all the Union battle victories.

When Johnson returned to Tennessee, he found that state leaders were now willing to do everything

President Lincoln thought Andrew Johnson would be an excellent running mate in 1864, because Johnson was a Southerner who was loyal to the Union.

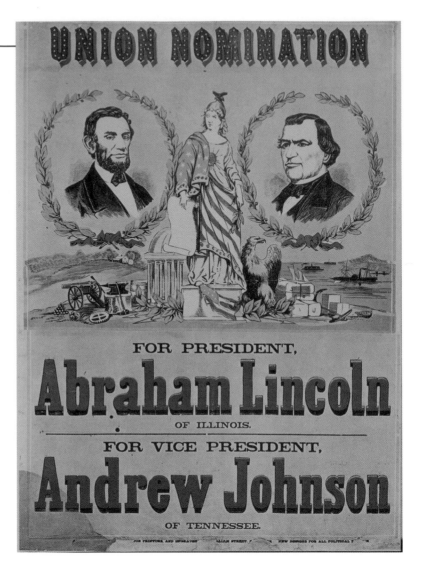

necessary to rejoin the United States. They promised to support the Constitution, the United States, and Union troops in the defeat of the Confederacy. They also voted to free the slaves and outlaw slavery in Tennessee.

On March 4, 1865, Andrew Johnson was sworn in as the vice president of the United States. He served in this role for only six weeks.

MILITARY GOVERNOR OF TENNESSEE

When the Union army invaded part of any Confederate state during the Civil War, President Lincoln appointed a military governor to take control. Andrew Johnson was the first to be chosen. In 1862, Lincoln made him a brigadier general and sent him to Nashville, Tennessee.

Johnson had a tough job. There was no state legislature to make the laws. He had to take charge of the government by himself. Most of the people in Nashville were loyal to the Confederacy. They hated all Unionists—and especially Johnson. He insisted that Confederates pledge their loyalty to the Union.

To make his job even harder, Nashville was in great danger from Confederate raiders. They attacked Unionists, exploded bridges, chopped up railroad ties, and blasted railroad tunnels. Despite the danger, Johnson stood his ground and held on to Nashville.

Many Tennessee leaders told Johnson that he was too hard on the Southern people. They said that his harsh rules made people hate the Union more. How would the people of Tennessee work together to rebuild their state after the war if there was so much hate?

Johnson did not listen to their advice. He refused to consider any compromise. He was sure that he was right to punish the Confederate traitors. After the war, it was very difficult for the people of Tennessee to work together.

CHAPTER THREE

RECONSTRUCTION

After four long years of war, the Confederate States of America finally surrendered in April 1865. The Civil War was over. Everywhere in the North, people celebrated. But in the South, people were devastated. The war was almost entirely fought on Southern soil. As a result, Southerners' homes, farms, businesses, and land were destroyed.

The United States government faced an enormous challenge. How should it handle the Southerners and their problems now that the war was over? Before the government could deal with this question, a terrible tragedy struck the nation. On April 14, 1865—just five days after the South surrendered—President Lincoln was assassinated.

A few hours after Lincoln died on April 15, Andrew Johnson took the oath of office. He was the president of the United States.

At first, Johnson vowed to punish the South for the war. But a few weeks later, he changed his mind. He realized that rebuilding the South could reunite the country. It also could make the United States stronger than ever. To achieve these goals, he knew

that the South needed help, not punishment. Hurting the South would only weaken the nation.

There was another reason that Johnson changed his mind. Even though the next presidential election was more than three years away, he was already planning for it. He would need Southern votes to be reelected president in 1868. He thought that if he helped the South, the Southerners would vote for him.

Johnson **pardoned** many Southerners who had helped the Confederacy. In return, these Southerners pledged their loyalty to the United States. Johnson's **reconstruction** plan helped the Southern states govern themselves again.

Johnson is shown seated at left in this painting of Lincoln's death. Actually, Johnson was not present at the time. Because Lincoln's wife Mary hated Johnson, he was asked to leave the room a few hours before the president died.

This photograph shows Richmond, Virginia, in 1865. After the war, much of the South was in ruins. Men, women, and children in every Southern state were starving. Many homes and buildings were destroyed.

John Wilkes Booth is known as the man who killed President Lincoln. But he is just one member of the group who plotted to assassinate him. When Booth shot Lincoln on April 14, 1865, George Atzerodt was supposed to kill Vice President Johnson. This plan failed because Atzerodt got so drunk, he never came near Johnson.

When Congress met in December of 1865, Johnson's reconstruction plan had been at work for months. The majority of Republicans in Congress—many of whom were from the North—did not like Johnson's plan. They believed that the South was to blame for the war and should suffer for it. They were also worried about the fate of the newly freed slaves. Wealthy Southerners had enslaved African Americans for centuries. Could they be trusted to guard the rights of the **freedpeople?** The Republicans didn't think so.

The Republicans had good reason to be concerned. By late 1865, the leaders of the Southern states were determined that white Southerners should have all the power. They wanted African Americans to be powerless. To achieve this goal, the Southern states, cities, and towns passed laws called the Black Codes. These laws limited the freedoms of African Americans. They determined things such as what kind of jobs African Americans could have and where they could live.

In 1866, Congress passed two laws to protect African Americans in the South. One arranged for some of the freedpeople to continue receiving food, education, and land. The other law was the Civil Rights Act of 1866. It declared that the ex-slaves were citizens of the United States and had all the rights of citizens.

President Johnson startled Congress by vetoing both bills. He said the laws were **unconstitutional**

In 1866, President Johnson took a train tour of Northern cities. He believed that if Northerners could hear him explain his ideas about the South and Reconstruction, they would agree with him. In each speech, however, the president was unable to control his anger at the Northern Republicans in Congress. People were dismayed to see the president act in this way. The tour was a failure.

This political cartoon shows Andrew Johnson as the tailor from Tennessee. He is sewing the states together to repair Uncle Sam's coat. Unfortunately, Johnson's plans to reunite the Union failed. Congress did not like his plans for Reconstruction.

African Americans in the South celebrated when the Civil Rights Act of 1866 became law. They hoped this event would change their lives for the better.

because they took away the rights of states to make their own laws. Republicans in Congress were angry about the vetoes. One group—the **Radical Republicans**—was especially upset. They never expected President Johnson to help the South and the ex-Confederates. After all, he had promised to punish the South! Congress voted to **override** the president's veto. The Civil Rights Act became the law of the land.

The Radical Republicans quickly realized the **Supreme Court** might decide that the Civil Rights Act was unconstitutional. So they prepared an **amendment** to the Constitution. Congress approved the new 14th Amendment, which guaranteed the right of citizenship of African Americans. It also kept ex-Confederates from being elected to political positions. As soon as three-quarters of the states voted to **ratify** it, the 14th Amendment would become law.

President Johnson believed the 14th Amendment was unconstitutional. He advised the Southern states

Andrew Johnson worked very hard as president, but his stubbornness often got in the way. He was so certain that he was right, he often refused to listen to advice or the opinions of others. He did not like to compromise with Congress. These qualities made it difficult for him to be a successful president.

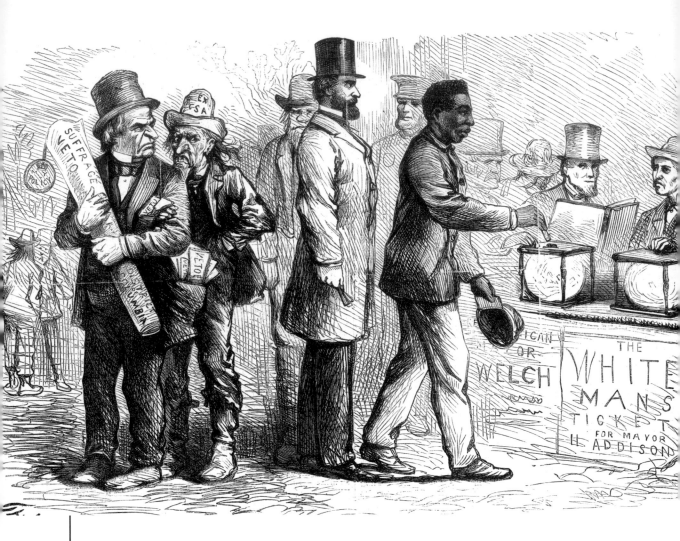

This 1867 political cartoon shows an African American man voting as Andrew Johnson looks on angrily.

not to ratify it. This made the Republicans even angrier. Johnson also believed that African Americans should be free, but he did not agree that they should have all the rights of white people. Like many white Americans in the 1860s, he had the mistaken belief that African Americans were not as capable or as smart as whites.

Northern Republicans believed that the freed slaves must have the right to vote. The ballot was crucial to their safety in the South, they said. If African

American men could not choose their leaders, then the white Southerners might try to take away all their rights and power.

President Johnson, like most white Americans in the North and South, did not agree. He wrongly believed that black people were not capable of making important decisions, such as voting. He was also convinced that black people needed white leaders to guide them. As a result, he allowed each state to decide whether African American men could vote or not. No Southern state allowed black men to vote. Several Northern states also voted against African Americans voting.

The Northern Republicans were very angry at President Johnson. How could he not support giving loyal black men the right to vote? After all, they had fought bravely for the Union in the Civil War. White Southerners, these Northerners said, had been disloyal by fighting against the United States.

The Radical Republicans won many victories in the November elections of 1866. Now the Republicans were in control of Congress. They could override the president's veto much more easily and pass the laws they wanted. They would make sure that the ex-Confederate leaders did not rule the South. They would protect African Americans from unjust laws and violence.

The Republicans replaced Johnson's reconstruction plan with one of their own. The Reconstruction Act of 1867 carved up the Southern states into five military

Johnson was a slave owner before slavery became illegal. At the beginning of the Civil War, he owned a man and a woman as well as two girls and a boy. Johnson did not turn against slavery until Lincoln issued the Emancipation Proclamation in 1863. This act was intended to free slaves in the South.

President Johnson was the first president to welcome a queen into the White House. Queen Emma of Hawaii visited the United States in August 1866.

In 1887, Congress overturned the Tenure of Office Act.

districts. A Northern general controlled each district. The generals made sure that each state wrote a new state constitution and formed a new government. Before a state could rejoin the United States, it had to allow African American men to vote. It also had to ratify the 14th Amendment. Soon the 15th Amendment would enforce the right of black men throughout the country to vote. (Women of all races could not vote until 1920.)

The Republicans in Congress passed two other laws. These bills limited the president's powers. The Tenure of Office Act made it illegal for the president to fire the members of his **cabinet** and other government officials. He had to get the approval of the Senate first. The other law made it illegal for the president to send his military orders directly to the army. First he had to send them to General Ulysses S. Grant, a Republican. President Johnson was furious about these two laws. After all, the Constitution did not give Congress the right to take away the powers of the president.

For some time, President Johnson had been unhappy with Edwin Stanton, the secretary of war in his cabinet. President Johnson decided to fire him and test the Tenure of Office Act. The Republicans decided that this action was the last straw. They vowed to do everything in their power to remove him from office. The battle was on!

AFRICAN AMERICANS— FREE AT LAST?

In December of 1865, the 13th Amendment to the Constitution was ratified. It guaranteed that the nation's four million slaves were forever free. No one in the United States could enslave African Americans ever again. But were they really free? What were their lives like after freedom?

After the war, many black families in the South wanted to own small farms, but white landowners refused to sell them land. Many whites also would not rent land to African Americans or give them bank loans. As a result, African Americans had no choice but to work for white farmers who barely paid them enough to feed their families.

White Southerners passed laws known as the Black Codes. These laws varied from state to state, but they all had one thing in common. They prevented African Americans from living as fully free people. They also made sure that whites had all the power and that blacks remained poor and landless. In some states, African Americans were allowed to work only as farm laborers and servants for white people. The law closed all other jobs to them. The African Americans in this picture were laborers who picked cotton for a white plantation owner. They were paid very little for this back-breaking work, and their new lives seemed little better than slavery.

Some Southern states had laws that prevented black people from traveling from one village to the next. This made it difficult for blacks to hold more than one job. In some places, children were forced to work without pay.

In spite of all their troubles, African Americans kept their courage. They built strong communities. They worshipped in their own churches and educated themselves and their children. And they waited for new laws that would allow them to be truly free.

CHAPTER FOUR

IMPEACHMENT!

When President Johnson violated the Tenure of Office Act, he disobeyed a law that Congress had passed. To the Radical Republicans, this meant the president had committed a crime and could be impeached. On February 24, 1868, the House of Representatives voted to impeach President Johnson by a vote of 128 to 47.

The House delivered 11 articles (reasons) for the impeachment. Most of the articles were connected to Johnson's firing of Secretary of War Edwin Stanton. Another article said that Johnson harmed Congress when he criticized it in his speeches.

According to the Constitution, Congress can impeach the president if he or she is guilty of "treason, **bribery,** or other high crimes and **misdemeanors."** The articles of impeachment did not accuse Johnson of treason or bribery. So the House considered his misdeeds to be in the category of "high

Andrew Johnson was the first president to be impeached.

crimes and misdemeanors." This is a difficult phrase to define because the Constitution does not explain what it means. Members of Congress must decide if a president's actions are serious enough to be considered "high crimes and misdemeanors."

Johnson was confident that he did not deserve to be impeached. He continued to work as if this cloud did not hang over him. He chose the best lawyers to defend him.

Johnson wanted to defend himself at his trial. On some days, he felt so frustrated that he wanted to march into the Senate and stand up for himself. Each time, his lawyers insisted that he remain at the White House.

After the Senate gave its reasons for the impeachment, the president's lawyers stated their case. They argued that Johnson could not be found guilty of violating the Tenure of Office Act. They explained that the law was unconstitutional. Not only that, but President Abraham Lincoln had appointed Stanton, not Johnson. The law did not even apply in this case.

On May 16, the senators voted on one article. Thirty-five senators voted to convict Johnson, or find him guilty. All of them were Republicans. Another 19 voted to **acquit** him, including seven Republicans. The senators did not have enough votes to convict President Johnson—they were one vote short! On May 26, the senators voted on two more articles. The results were exactly the same. They were still one vote short. The Senate then voted to end the trial. President Johnson was acquitted! He could now finish his term. He also could campaign for his reelection.

In the spring of 1868, the nation was buzzing with talk about President Johnson's impeachment. Newspapers were full of articles, pictures, and stories about the trial. Crowds of people jammed the galleries of Congress, eager to witness the startling events.

Why did the impeachment trial fail to convict Johnson? There were many reasons, but one was very important. Some senators (even some Republicans) realized that if Johnson were convicted, any future president who disagreed with Congress might be forced out of office. This would harm the nation. The Constitution gives the president the right to disagree with Congress when he believes it is wrong. This is why the Constitution gives the president the power to veto the laws that Congress makes.

President Johnson was disappointed when the Democratic Party did not choose him as their candidate for president in 1868. He had less than a year left to be president. In spite of all his battles with Congress, he still achieved some important goals. For example, he approved the plan to purchase Alaska from Russia.

Tickets were sold to citizens who wanted to attend the impeachment trial of President Johnson.

Many Southerners celebrated when Johnson was acquitted. They fired off guns, had firework displays, and held parties.

In 1867, Secretary of State William Seward purchased Alaska from Russia for about $7 million. Newspapers joked about it. This political cartoon shows an American politician trying unsuccessfully to find voters in Alaska.

When President Johnson was elected senator in 1874, nearly six years had passed since he was in the White House. He was filled with joy when his victory was announced. He believed that the vote meant that he had been a good president, in spite of his impeachment. He declared, "I'd rather have this information than to learn that I had been elected President of the United States!"

The Alaska Purchase in 1867 would prove to be a momentous addition to the United States. Secretary of State William Henry Seward was an important member of President Johnson's cabinet. He had been eager to buy Alaska for the United States ever since he took office. In 1866, Russia was ready to sell the vast territory.

On March 30, 1867, President Johnson signed the treaty to purchase Alaska for $7.2 million dollars. This meant that the United States bought Alaska for about two cents an acre! Many people, however, believed that Alaska was a foolhardy purchase. At that time, no one knew that Alaska was so rich in timber, fish, oil, gold, and other minerals. Some people made fun of both President Johnson and Secretary Seward. They called Alaska "Johnson's Polar Bear Garden," "Seward's Folly," and "Seward's Ice Box."

President Johnson is also remembered because he tried to make peace with Native Americans in the West.

He also successfully removed the French government from Mexico. This was a big accomplishment because the United States had hoped for years to remove all European powers from the Americas. Johnson also continued to pardon Southerners. On December 25, 1868, he pardoned all the ex-Confederates.

When Johnson returned to Tennessee in March 1869, he stayed active in politics. In 1874, he was elected U.S. senator. He returned to Washington, D.C., in 1875 but served only a few months. On a trip to Tennessee, he suffered a stroke. He died a few days later, on July 31, 1875. He was 66 years old.

On March 20, 1875, Senator Johnson spoke to his fellow senators for the last time. His final words were, "May God bless this people, may God save the Constitution."

After President Johnson's death, newspapers in both the North and the South printed articles about his contributions to the country. Northern newspapers focused on Johnson's loyalty to the Union during the Civil War. Southern newspapers pointed to the president's work to help the South during Reconstruction.

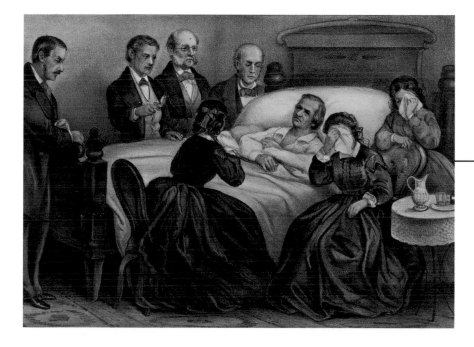

Johnson continued to serve his country until the end of his life. He died while visiting his daughter Mary in Carter County, Tennessee, in 1875.

WHAT IS IMPEACHMENT?

When the United States was a new nation, the men who wrote the Constitution understood that someday a president might be involved in a crime or might do something so wrong that he should no longer be president. The Constitution gives Congress the power to: 1. impeach the president, 2. put him on trial, 3. convict him, and 4. remove him from office. This is how the impeachment process works:

According to the Constitution, if a majority of members of the House of Representatives vote that they believe the president has committed "treason, bribery, or other high crimes and misdemeanors," then they have impeached the president. Two presidents have been impeached, Andrew Johnson in 1868 and William Clinton in 1998. In 1974, President Richard Nixon resigned before the House voted to impeach him.

Once the House has impeached the president, the Senate must put the president on trial. During the trial, the Senate presents evidence of the president's wrongdoing. The president's lawyers defend his actions. Then the senators vote. If two-thirds or more of the senators vote to convict him, then the president must be removed from office. If fewer than two-thirds of the senators vote to convict, then the president is acquitted and remains in office. The Constitution also allows Congress to impeach the vice president and other "civil officers of the United States." Civil officers include judges and other important government officials.

THE FIRST LADY
AND FIRST DAUGHTER

When Eliza Johnson became the First Lady in 1865, she had never been to Washington, D.C. She had always lived in Tennessee. The move to the White House was difficult for her because she was ill with **tuberculosis**. Her poor health prevented her from being an active hostess like most First Ladies. Fortunately, her older daughter, Martha Johnson Patterson, moved to Washington soon after Johnson became president. She was the wife of Tennessee Senator David T. Patterson. She agreed to act as her father's hostess at parties and receptions. When she was unable to help, her younger sister Mary was sometimes available.

Eliza Johnson

Yet Mrs. Johnson was very important to her husband while he was president. He met with her each morning and evening. They usually discussed the issues and events of his day. She was well-informed about national events because she read many newspapers and magazines. She helped him by clipping news articles and gluing them into scrapbooks. She also guarded his health and tried to make sure he got a good night's sleep. In the evening, before bed, she showed him only good news articles that praised his actions. Only in the morning would she show him articles that disagreed with him.

Martha Johnson Patterson

| 1800 | 1810 | 1820 | 1830 | 1840 |

1808
Andrew Johnson is born in Raleigh, North Carolina on December 29.

1812
Jacob Johnson, Andrew Johnson's father, dies.

1822
At age 13, Johnson becomes an apprentice to James Selby, a tailor in Raleigh. He joins his older brother William, who is already an apprentice.

1824
The Johnson brothers leave their apprenticeships and run away from Raleigh.

1826
Johnson settles in East Tennessee.

1827
Johnson marries Eliza McCardle of Greeneville, Tennessee. Johnson sets up his own tailor shop.

1829
Johnson is elected alderman in Greeneville. He is reelected in 1830 and 1831.

1834
Johnson is elected mayor of Greeneville.

1835
Johnson is elected as a representative to the Tennessee state legislature. He travels to Nashville to serve his term.

1837
Johnson is not reelected to the state legislature. Once more, he is elected mayor of Greeneville.

1839
Johnson is reelected to the Tennessee state legislature.

1841
Johnson wins his campaign for state senator.

1843
Johnson is elected to the U.S. House of Representatives.

1845
After a bitter, difficult campaign, Johnson is reelected to the House.

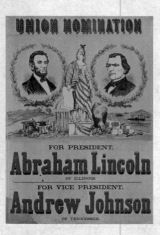

UNION NOMINATION

FOR PRESIDENT,
Abraham Lincoln
OF ILLINOIS

FOR VICE PRESIDENT,
Andrew Johnson
OF TENNESSEE

1852
The House of Representatives accepts Johnson's homestead bill, but the Senate later votes against it. It does not become a law.

1853
Johnson loses his seat in the House but is elected governor of Tennessee.

1855
Johnson is reelected governor of Tennessee.

1857
Johnson is elected a U.S. senator. When he arrives in Washington, D.C., he again works on his homestead bill.

1860
The House and Senate pass Johnson's homestead bill, but President Buchanan vetoes it. Johnson wants to run for president but finally decides against it. In December, South Carolina is the first state to secede from the United States.

1861
In February and March, Johnson demands that the Southern states remain in the Union. On April 12, the Civil War begins. Johnson fails to convince the people of Tennessee to remain in the Union. Tennessee joins the Confederacy on June 8. Johnson returns to the U.S. Senate.

1862
In March, President Lincoln appoints Johnson the military governor of Tennessee. Johnson returns to Nashville.

1863
Johnson struggles to govern Tennessee because most of its citizens are Confederates.

1864
Lincoln selects Johnson to be the candidate for vice president. In November, President Lincoln and Johnson win the election.

1865
On March 4, Johnson is inaugurated vice president. General Robert E. Lee's Army of Northern Virginia surrenders on April 9. The Confederacy falls soon after. On April 14, Johnson visits Lincoln at the White House. They discuss plans for the reconstruction of the South. That night, Lincoln is shot at Ford's Theater. On April 15, Lincoln dies. Johnson is sworn in as the 17th president. Johnson carries out his own reconstruction plan in the South. He pardons many ex-Confederates. In December, the 13th Amendment becomes law. The Constitution now guarantees the freedom of all African Americans.

1866
Congress approves two bills to help African Americans in the South. Johnson vetoes both laws. Congress overrides both vetoes, and the bills become laws. In the fall, Johnson campaigns throughout the North for the Democrats. He criticizes the Republicans in his speeches and turns many Northerners against him. In November, the Republicans win more seats in Congress.

1867
Republicans are now in control of Congress. They toss out Johnson's reconstruction plan and enact one of their own. They prepare a 14th Amendment to protect the rights of African Americans. President Johnson approves the purchase of Alaska. He successfully removes the French government from Mexico, an important achievement for the United States.

1868
The House of Representatives impeaches Johnson. The Senate puts Johnson on trial. Johnson is acquitted. The 14th Amendment is ratified and becomes law. The Democratic Party does not choose Johnson as its candidate for president.

1869
In March, Johnson ends his term of office. He returns to Greeneville, Tennessee.

1875
Johnson returns to Washington to serve in the U.S. Senate. He becomes the only former president to serve in the Senate. He dies several months later of a stroke.

GLOSSARY

acquit (uh-KWIT) When public officials acquit a person, they decide he or she is not guilty of a crime. The Senate had to acquit President Johnson because they did not have enough votes to convict him.

amendment (uh-MEND-ment) An amendment is a change or addition to the Constitution or other documents. The 14th Amendment guaranteed the rights of African Americans.

apprentices (uh-PREN-tis-iz) Apprentices are people who learn a skill under the teaching of an expert worker. As an apprentice, Johnson learned to be a tailor.

assassinate (uh-SASS-uh-nayt) To assassinate means to murder someone, especially a well-known person. Some people threatened to assassinate Senator Johnson.

bill (BILL) A bill is an idea for a new law that is presented to a group of lawmakers. Johnson proposed a bill that later became the Homestead Act.

bribery (BRY-bur-ee) Bribery is when a person offers money or another reward to others, hoping to encourage them to do something in exchange. The Constitution states that bribery is a cause for impeachment.

cabinet (KAB-ih-net) A cabinet is the group of people who advise a president. The Tenure of Office Act made it illegal for a president to fire members of his cabinet.

candidate (KAN-dih-det) A candidate is a person running in an election. The Republican Party selected Johnson as the candidate for vice president in the election of 1864.

compromise (KOM-pruh-myz) A compromise is a way to settle a disagreement in which both sides give up part of what they want. President Johnson refused to compromise on many issues.

Confederacy (kun-FED-ur-uh-see) The Confederacy is another name for the Confederate States of America. The Confederacy included all the Southern states that seceded from the Union.

constable (KON-stuh-bul) A constable is like a police officer. Andrew Johnson's father was a constable.

constitution (kon-stih-TOO-shun) A constitution is the set of basic principles that govern a state, country, or society. Johnson promised to protect the U.S. Constitution.

debating (dih-BAY-ting) Debating means taking part in a contest in which opponents argue for opposite sides of an issue. Johnson enjoyed debating.

Democrat (DEM-uh-krat) A Democrat is a member of the Democratic Party, one of the two major political parties in the United States. Johnson, like many Southerners of his day, was a Democrat.

freedpeople (FREED-pee-pul) The freedpeople were African Americans who had been slaves before slavery became illegal. The Radical Republicans passed laws to help the freedpeople in the South.

homestead (HOME-sted) A homestead is a piece of land settled by a family. Johnson believed that a homestead would provide a poor man with a living and a way to gain wealth. The Homestead Act gave anyone who was 21 years old and the head of a household 160 acres if that person lived on and made improvements to the land over a five-year period. Only a filing fee of 18 dollars was required.

impeach (im-PEECH) If the House of Representatives votes to impeach a president, it charges him or her with a crime or serious misdeed. The House decided to impeach Johnson because he violated a law, the Tenure of Office Act.

misdemeanors (mis-dee-MEE-nurz) Misdemeanors are wrongful actions that are considered less serious than actual crimes. At Andrew Johnson's trial, his lawyers argued that his deeds were neither crimes nor misdemeanors.

override (oh-vur-RIDE) When people override something, they cancel it or set it aside. In 1866, the Civil Rights Act became a law when the Senate decided to override the president's veto.

pardon (PAR-den) When leaders pardon people, they excuse them for their crimes or misdeeds. Johnson pardoned thousands of Confederates after the Civil War.

political parties (puh-LIT-uh-kul PAR-teez) Political parties are groups of people who share similar ideas about how to run a government. Lincoln and Johnson were from different political parties, but they were both Unionists.

politics (PAWL-uh-tiks) Politics refers to the actions and practices of the government. Johnson had a long career in politics.

Radical Republicans (RAD-ih-kul ree-PUB-lih-kenz) The Radical Republicans were a group of Northern Republicans that wanted a severe form of reconstruction in the South. The Radical Republicans were determined that the ex-Confederates should suffer and struggle before they rejoined the United States.

ratify (RAT-ih-fy) If something is ratified, it is approved by a group of people. If three-quarters of the states ratify an amendment to the Constitution, it becomes law.

reconstruction (ree-kun-STRUK-shun) Reconstruction is the rebuilding of something. Johnson's reconstruction plan helped the Southern states govern themselves again after the Civil War.

Republican (ree-PUB-lih-ken) A Republican is a member of the Republican Party, one of the two major political parties in the United States. In Johnson's time, many Republicans were against slavery.

secede (suh-SEED) If a group secedes, it separates from a larger group. The southern states seceded from the Union to form their own country after Lincoln was elected in 1860.

state legislature (STAYT LEJ-uh-slay-chur) The state legislature is the part of state government that makes the laws. Johnson wanted to help working people when he served in the Tennessee state legislature.

Supreme Court (suh-PREEM KORT) The Supreme Court is the most powerful court in the United States. The Supreme Court decides if a law is unconstitutional.

treason (TREE-zen) Treason is a crime against the government of a nation. Andrew Johnson believed that Confederates were guilty of treason against the United States.

tuberculosis (tu-bur-kyuh-LOH-siss) Tuberculosis is a highly contagious bacterial disease that usually affects the lungs.

unconstitutional (un-kon-stih-TOO-shuh-nel) If a law is unconstitutional, it violates or goes against the laws and ideas in the Constitution. The Supreme Court decides if something is unconstitutional.

Unionists (YOON-yen-istz) Unionists were people who supported the Union during the Civil War. Even though he was a Southerner, Andrew Johnson was a Unionist.

veto (VEE-toh) A veto is the president's power to refuse to sign a bill into law. Andrew Johnson decided to veto bills that he believed were unconstitutional.

THE UNITED STATES GOVERNMENT

The United States government is divided into three equal branches: the executive, the legislative, and the judicial. This division helps prevent abuses of power because each branch has to answer to the other two. No one branch can become too powerful.

EXECUTIVE BRANCH

President
Vice President
Departments

The job of the executive branch is to enforce the laws. It is headed by the president, who serves as the spokesperson for the United States around the world. The president signs bills into law and appoints important officials such as federal judges. He or she is also the commander in chief of the U.S. military. The president is assisted by the vice president, who takes over if the president dies or cannot carry out the duties of the office.

The executive branch also includes various departments, each focused on a specific topic. They include the Defense Department, the Justice Department, and the Agriculture Department. The department heads, along with other officials such as the vice president, serve as the president's closest advisers, called the cabinet.

LEGISLATIVE BRANCH

Congress
Senate and
House of Representatives

The job of the legislative branch is to make the laws. It consists of Congress, which is divided into two parts: the Senate and the House of Representatives. The Senate has 100 members, and the House of Representatives has 435 members. Each state has two senators. The number of representatives a state has varies depending on the state's population.

Besides making laws, Congress also passes budgets and enacts taxes. In addition, it is responsible for declaring war, maintaining the military, and regulating trade with other countries.

JUDICIAL BRANCH

Supreme Court
Courts of Appeals
District Courts

The job of the judicial branch is to interpret the laws. It consists of the nation's federal courts. Trials are held in district courts. During trials, judges must decide what laws mean and how they apply. Courts of appeals review the decisions made in district courts.

The nation's highest court is the Supreme Court. If someone disagrees with a court of appeals ruling, he or she can ask the Supreme Court to review it. The Supreme Court may refuse. The Supreme Court makes sure that decisions and laws do not violate the Constitution.

CHOOSING
THE PRESIDENT

It may seem odd, but American voters don't elect the president directly. Instead, the president is chosen using what is called the Electoral College.

Each state gets as many votes in the Electoral College as its combined total of senators and representatives in Congress. For example, Iowa has two senators and five representatives, so it gets seven electoral votes. Although the District of Columbia does not have any voting members in Congress, it gets three electoral votes. Usually, the candidate who wins the most votes in any given state receives all of that state's electoral votes.

To become president, a candidate must get more than half of the Electoral College votes. There are a total of 538 votes in the Electoral College, so a candidate needs 270 votes to win. If nobody receives 270 Electoral College votes, the House of Representatives chooses the president.

With the Electoral College system, the person who receives the most votes nationwide does not always receive the most electoral votes. This happened most recently in 2000, when Al Gore received half a million more national votes than George W. Bush. Bush became president because he had more Electoral College votes.

THE WHITE HOUSE

The White House is the official home of the president of the United States. It is located at 1600 Pennsylvania Avenue NW in Washington, D.C. In 1792, a contest was held to select the architect who would design the president's home. James Hoban won. Construction took eight years.

The first president, George Washington, never lived in the White House. The second president, John Adams, moved into the house in 1800, though the inside was not yet complete. During the War of 1812, British soldiers burned down much of the White House. It was rebuilt several years later.

The White House was changed through the years. Porches were added, and President Theodore Roosevelt added the West Wing. President William Taft changed the shape of the presidential office, making it into the famous Oval Office. While Harry Truman was president, the old house was discovered to be structurally weak. All the walls were reinforced with steel, and the rooms were rebuilt.

Today, the White House has 132 rooms (including 35 bathrooms), 28 fireplaces, and 3 elevators. It takes 570 gallons of paint to cover the outside of the six-story building. The White House provides the president with many ways to relax. It includes a putting green, a jogging track, a swimming pool, a tennis court, and beautifully landscaped gardens. The White House also has a movie theater, a billiard room, and a one-lane bowling alley.

PRESIDENTIAL PERKS

The job of president of the United States is challenging. It is probably one of the most stressful jobs in the world. Because of this, presidents are paid well, though not nearly as well as the leaders of large corporations. In 2007, the president earned $400,000 a year. Presidents also receive extra benefits that make the demanding job a little more appealing.

★ **Camp David:** In the 1940s, President Franklin D. Roosevelt chose this heavily wooded spot in the mountains of Maryland to be the presidential retreat, where presidents can relax. Even though it is a retreat, world business is conducted there. Most famously, President Jimmy Carter met with Middle Eastern leaders at Camp David in 1978. The result was a peace agreement between Israel and Egypt.

★ *Air Force One*: The president flies on a jet called *Air Force One*. It is a Boeing 747-200B that has been modified to meet the president's needs.

Air Force One is the size of a large home. It is equipped with a dining room, sleeping quarters, a conference room, and office space. It also has two kitchens that can provide food for up to 50 people.

★ **The Secret Service:** While not the most glamorous of the president's perks, the Secret Service is one of the most important. The Secret Service is a group of highly trained agents who protect the president and the president's family.

★ **The Presidential State Car:** The presidential limousine is a stretch Cadillac DTS.

It has been armored to protect the president in case of attack. Inside the plush car are a foldaway desk, an entertainment center, and a communications console.

★ **The Food:** The White House has five chefs who will make any food the president wants. The White House also has an extensive wine collection.

★ **Retirement:** A former president receives a pension, or retirement pay, of just under $180,000 a year. Former presidents also receive Secret Service protection for the rest of their lives.

FACTS

QUALIFICATIONS

To run for president, a candidate must

★ be at least 35 years old
★ be a citizen who was born in the United States
★ have lived in the United States for 14 years

TERM OF OFFICE

A president's term of office is four years.
No president can stay in office for more than two terms.

ELECTION DATE

The presidential election takes place every four years on the first Tuesday of November.

INAUGURATION DATE

Presidents are inaugurated on January 20.

OATH OF OFFICE

I do solemnly swear I will faithfully execute the office of the President of the United States and will to the best of my ability preserve, protect, and defend the Constitution of the United States.

WRITE A LETTER TO THE PRESIDENT

One of the best things about being a U.S. citizen is that Americans get to participate in their government. They can speak out if they feel government leaders aren't doing their jobs. They can also praise leaders who are going the extra mile. Do you have something you'd like the president to do? Should the president worry more about the environment and encourage people to recycle? Should the government spend more money on our schools? You can write a letter to the president to say how you feel!

1600 Pennsylvania Avenue
Washington, D.C. 20500
You can even send an e-mail to: president@whitehouse.gov

BOOKS

Flanagan, Timothy. *Reconstruction: A Primary Source History of the Struggle to Unite the North and South after the Civil War.* New York: Rosen Publishing Group, 2005.

Havelin, Kate. *Andrew Johnson.* Minneapolis, MN.: Lerner, 2004.

Nardo, Don. *Andrew Johnson: America's Seventeenth President.* New York: Children's Press, 2004.

Ruggiero, Adriane. *Reconstruction.* New York: Marshall Cavendish Benchmark, 2006.

Shea, Peggi Dietz. *The Impeachment Process.* New York: Chelsea House, 2000.

VIDEOS

Aftershock: Beyond the Civil War. DVD (New York: A & E Home Video, 2007).

The American President. DVD, VHS (Alexandria, VA: PBS Home Video, 2000).

The History Channel Presents The President. DVD (New York: A & E Home Video, 2005).

National Geographic's Inside the White House. DVD (Washington, D.C.: National Geographic Video, 2003).

Reconstruction: The Second Civil War. DVD (Alexandria, VA: PBS Home Video, 2004).

INTERNET SITES

Visit our Web page for lots of links about Andrew Johnson and other U.S. presidents:

http://www.childsworld.com/links

Note to Parents, Teachers, and Librarians: We routinely verify our Web links to make sure they are safe, active sites—so encourage your readers to check them out!

INDEX